Enough of Him

May Sumbwanyambe

methuen | drama

LONDON • NEW YORK • OXFORD • NEW DELHI • SYDNEY

METHUEN DRAMA
Bloomsbury Publishing Plc
50 Bedford Square, London, WC1B 3DP, UK
1385 Broadway, New York, NY 10018, USA
29 Earlsfort Terrace, Dublin 2, Ireland

BLOOMSBURY, METHUEN DRAMA and the Methuen
Drama logo are trademarks of Bloomsbury Publishing Plc

First published in Great Britain 2022

Cover photography © Tommy Ga-Ken Wan

A catalogue record for this book is available from the British Library.

A catalog record for this book is available from the Library of Congress.

ISBN: PB: 978-1-3503-7775-2
ePDF: 978-1-3503–7776-9
eBook: 978-1-3503-7777-6

Series: Modern Plays

Typeset by Mark Heslington Ltd, Scarborough, North Yorkshire

To find out more about our authors and books visit
www.bloomsbury.com and sign up for our newsletters.

CREATIVE TEAM

Emma Jones	Lighting Designer
Ingrid Mackinnon	Movement Director and Intimacy Director
Ana Beatriz Meireles	Associate Movement Director and Associate Intimacy Director
Fred Meller	Set and Costume Designer
Pippa Murphy	Sound Designer
Orla O'Loughlin	Director
John Pfumojena	Composer
May Sumbwanyambe	Writer
Garen Abel Unokan	Associate Director

TECHNICAL TEAM

Peter Fennell	Lighting and Sound Manager (Pitlochry)
Alice Black	Production Manager (Tour)
Julie Carlin	Wardrobe Manager (Pitlochry)
Roger Collins	Company Stage Manager
Deborah Dickinson	Producer (Pitlochry)
Iona Fterman	Senior Cutter (Pitlochry)
Peter Fennell	Lighting and Sound Manager (Pitlochry)
Elise Frost	Stage Management placement
Robert Gear	Workshop Manager (Pitlochry)
Nina Madriz	Deputy Stage Manager
Dino Melia	Assistant Production Manager (Pitlochry)
Natalie Mitchell	Wardrobe Assistant / Cutter (Pitlochry)
Nick Trueman	Head of Production (Pitlochry)
Mike Whalley	Technical Manager (Pitlochry)
Annie Winton	Assistant Stage Manager

CAST

Omar Austin	Joseph Knight
Catriona Faint	Ann 'Annie' Thompson
Rachael-Rose McLaren	Margaret Wedderburn
Matthew Pidgeon	Sir John Wedderburn

ACCESS

Jacqui Beckford	BSL Interpreter
Chris McKiddie	Audio Describer
Glenda Carson	Captioner

A list of the National Theatre of Scotland staff involved in this and all productions can be found here: nationaltheatrescotland.com/about/contact-us

May Sumbwanyambe's research into Joseph Knight also informed a play for BBC Radio 4, *The Trial of Joseph Knight*.

May Sumbwanyambe | Writer

May Sumbwanyambe is a librettist, radio dramatist, academic and playwright from Edinburgh.

For National Theatre of Scotland: *Ghost Light* (Edinburgh International Festival and National Theatre of Scotland); *Joseph Knight* (BBC Scotland, National Theatre of Scotland).

Other work includes: *After Independence* (Arcola Theatre, Papatango Theatre); *The Parrot House* (Guildhall School of Music and Drama); *After Independence* and *The Trial of Joseph Knight* (BBC Radio 4).

He is currently writing new stage plays for the National Theatre of Scotland, the Citizens Theatre and Grid Iron Theatre Company/ National Trust for Scotland, all are about the historical visibility of Black peoples in Scotland. He is also developing a new TV series for Two Rivers Media/the BBC and a new radio play for BBC Radio 4.

In 2016 May's debut play was the winner of the Alfred Fagon Audience Award. He was the inaugural Papatango Resident Playwright and winner of the £10k BBC Performing Arts Opera Fellowship. Other award recognition includes being shortlisted for the Channel 4/Oran Mor Comedy Drama Award (2012), the Papatango New Writing Prize (2012), the Alfred Fagon Award (2011, 2012, 2015), the BBC's Alfred Bradley Award (2011) and OffWestEnd's Adopt a Playwright Award (2010 and 2009), the Old Vic 12 award (2016), Perfect Pitch £12k musical award (2016), IASH/Traverse Fellowship (2017, 2018), Live Theatre/Northumbria University Writer in Residence (2018) and the Dr Gavin Wallace Fellowship (2018). He also reached the final round of Soho Theatre's Verity Bargate Award (2011) and won the BBC's inaugural Scriptroom competition (2012).

Orla O'Loughlin | Director

Orla has directed an eclectic mix of award-winning and internationally acclaimed work at a range of theatres, festivals and non-conventional performance spaces including: the Young Vic, Royal Court, Hampstead Theatre, Traverse, Citizens, Tron, Tramway, Abbey Theatre, Project Theatre, Leeds Playhouse, Sherman Theatre, Theatre Royal Stratford East, B.A.C, 59E59 NYC, Edinburgh, Toronto, São Paulo, Spoleto, Melbourne, Adelaide, Auckland and Dublin International Festivals and in the West End.

Recent directing credits include: the multi-award winning productions *What Girls Are Made Of* (Traverse, Soho, Assembly, UK and international tour) and *Mouthpiece* (Traverse, Soho, international tour).

Orla is former Artistic Director of the Traverse Theatre and Associate Director of the Royal Court and is currently Vice Principal and Director of Drama at Guildhall School of Music and Drama where she was conferred the title Professor in recognition of her 'outstanding contribution to the advancement of her discipline'.

She is a recipient of the James Menzies Kitchin Award and the Carlton Award at the Donmar Warehouse. Orla was listed in the *Observer* as one of the top fifty cultural leaders in the UK and included in *The List* Top 20 Women in the Arts.

Garen Abel Unokan | Associate Director

Raised in South London but now Edinburgh based, Garen's writing has appeared in publications such as *The New Yorker* and *Black Ballad*; she is currently working on her first novel. As an artist, Garen is particularly interested in narratives surrounding queerness, Blackness, coming of age, and autonomy.

Directorial credits include: *Can I Touch Your Hair?* by Lekhani Chirwa (Vault Festival, 2019); *Glutathione* by Winsome Pinnock (Replay: Young Vic, 2019) and *Blend.Share.Mix* by Roli Okorodudu (Rapid Write Response at Theatre503, 2019).

Assisting credits include: *Jacaranda* by Lorna French and directed by Elle While (a Pentabus and Theatre By The Lake co-production, 2021) and *An Unfinished Man* by Dipo Baruwa-Etti and directed by Taio Lawson (The Yard, 2022).

Emma Jones | Lighting Designer

Emma is a Lighting Designer based in Scotland, working across the UK and abroad.

Emma has lit shows for numerous companies including Dundee Rep Theatre, Perth Theatre, Derby Theatre, Scottish Dance Theatre, Stellar Quines, The National Theatre of Scotland, The Royal Lyceum Edinburgh, Catherine Wheels Theatre Company and The Citizens

Theatre Glasgow. Recently Emma has started collaborating with music artist SHHE.

Emma has designed the lighting for over sixteen newly commissioned works for Scottish Dance Theatre and in 2020 became an associate artist with Shotput Theatre Company.

Ingrid Mackinnon | Movement Director and Intimacy Director

Ingrid Mackinnon is a London-based movement director and choreographer.

Movement direction credits include: *A Dead Body In Taos* (Fuel Theatre); *The Darkest Part of the Night* (Kiln Theatre); *Girl on an Altar* (Kiln Theatre); *Playboy of the West Indies* (Birmingham Rep); *The Meaning of Zong* (Bristol Old Vic/UK tour); *Moreno* (Theatre503); *Red Riding Hood* (Theatre Royal Stratford East); *Antigone* (Mercury Theatre); *Romeo and Juliet* (Regent's Park Open Air Theatre – winner Black British Theatre Awards 2021 Best Choreography); *Liminal – Le Gateau Chocolat* (King's Head Theatre); *Liar Heretic Thief* (Lyric Hammersmith); *Reimagining Cacophony* (Almeida Theatre); *First Encounters: The Merchant Of Venice, Kingdom Come* (RSC); *Josephine* (Theatre Royal Bath); *Typical* (Soho Theatre); *#WeAreArrested* (Arcola Theatre and RSC); *The Border* (Theatre Centre); *Fantastic Mr Fox* (as associate movement director, Nuffield Southampton and National/International tour); *Hamlet, #DR@CULA!* (Royal Central School of Speech and Drama); *Bonnie and Clyde* (UWL: London College of Music).

Other credits include: intimacy support for *Antigone, 101 Dalmatians*, *Legally Blonde, Carousel* (Regent's Park Open Air Theatre); intimacy director for *Girl on An Altar* (Kiln Theatre).

Ana Beatriz Meireles | Associate Movement Director and Associate Intimacy Director

Ana is a movement director, teacher and dance creative. She has worked professionally with companies including the Renaud Wiser Dance Company, Cascade Dance Theatre and KWAM Collective, and organisations such as the Young Vic and the National Theatre. Ana's movement direction work is influenced by her professional experience in contemporary dance and theatre settings, her expertise in functional movement and interest in somatic approaches.

Movement direction credits include: *Playtime* (Royal & Derngate); *Beat Poetry* (Rose Bruford South West); *Barricade* (BFI funded short film); *Sleepwalking* (Hampstead Theatre); *The Cosmonaut's Last Message* (GSA); *Hamlet* (Royal Central School of Speech and Drama) and *The Runner* (Greenwich Theatre R&D). As movement associate: *Red Riding Hood* (Stratford East). As co-choreographer: *EYE-I* (London Studio Centre).

She holds a BA (Hons) Dance Theatre degree from UAL and an MA in Movement: Directing and Teaching from the Royal Central School of Speech and Drama.

Fred Meller | Set and Costume Designer

Fred works on productions that are representative of devised, collaborative, and new writing agendas. Storytelling and story making in socially engaged practice to hear untold stories of marginalised or unseen voices are a consistent theme in Fred's performance practices. Fred has exhibited at The Prague Quadrennial and their work is also part of the V&A Museum permanent collection.

Fred is Director for Performance at Central Saint Martins, University of the Arts, London, and distinguished visiting professor at Tokyo University of the Arts.

Theatre credits include: *Gut, Meet Me At Dawn*, *Grain in the Blood*, *Milk*, *Swallow* (Traverse Theatre); *A Number* (Edinburgh Lyceum Theatre, Nominated for a 2017 Cat Award); *A Few Man Fridays* (Cardboard Citizens, The Riverside Studios); *Black Comedy* (The Watermill Theatre); *Woyzeck* (Cardboard Citizens, Southwark Playhouse); *Alaska* (Royal Court); *Timon of Athens* (RSC, Cardboard Citizens and The Complete Works Festival: London, Stratford, Belfast, Southampton); *The Fever* (Young Vic); *Pericles* (RSC, Cardboard Citizens); *The Whizz Kid* (Almeida); *The Visitation of Mr Collioni* (Platform Four Theatre Company, Salisbury Playhouse); *Life with an Idiot* (The Gate Theatre, National Theatre Studio); *Variety* (Grid Iron, Edinburgh International Festival); *Caledonian Road* (Almeida, site-specific).

Film credits include: *Here for Life* (Artangel, as Production Designer).

Pippa Murphy | Sound Designer

Pippa Murphy is an award-winning composer and sound designer who scores for film, theatre and dance.

For National Theatre Scotland: *Orphans*, *Total Immediate Collective Imminent Terrestrial Salvation* (Edinburgh International Festival, Royal Court and Tim Crouch); *Joseph Knight* (BBC); *Aleister Crowley* (BBC).

Theatre credits include: *Truth's a Dog* (Royal Lyceum Theatre); *An Edinburgh Christmas Carol* (Royal Lyceum Theatre); *Lost at Sea* (Perth Horsecross); *Wind Resistance* (Royal Lyceum Theatre); *Creditors* (Royal Lyceum Theatre); *A Streetcar Named Desire, Red Lion* (Rapture Theatre); *Woman in Mind* (Dundee Rep); *Crude* (Grid Iron); *Gilt* (7:84); *Strangers Babies* (Traverse Theatre); *Standing Wave* (Tron Theatre Glasgow).

Other credits include: *Message from the Skies* (Edinburgh Hogmanay 2020, 2019, 2018); *Anamchara – Songs of Friendship* (Scottish Opera, Commonwealth Games 2014); *POP-UP Duets* (Janis Claxton Dance, National Museums of Scotland); numerous arrangements and commissions (BBC Proms, BBC Scottish Symphony Orchestra, Scottish Chamber Orchestra, Dunedin Consort, GSA Choir, RGBE).

John Pfumojena | Composer

John Pfumojena trained in Inclusive Performance (BA Hons) at Chickenshed. He is a Visiting Fellow at the University of Oxford, a composer and songwriter with Warner Chappell Music, Trustee of Prime Theatre and an Associate Artist of Tangle Theatre.

Composer: *Richard the Second* (Tangle Theatre, in association with Mayflower/MAST Studios); *Bunker of Zion* (John Pfumojena, The Old Courts, Collaborative Touring Network); *The Jungle* (The Curran, San Francisco, St Anne's, Brooklyn, Playhouse Theatre, West End, Young Vic); *Dr Faustus* (Tangle Theatre), additional composition Beasty Baby (Theatre- Rites/Polka Theatre); *Colours* (Chipawo, Zimbabwe) and *Dream* (Ignite Africa Festival).

Music Director: *Richard the Second* (Tangle Theatre, in association with Mayflower/MAST Studios); *Bunker of Zion* (John Pfumojena, The Old Courts, Collaborative Touring Network); *For Black Boys* (The Royal Court, New Diorama Theatre); *The Jungle* (Good Chance Theatre,

National Theatre, Young Vic); *Junkyard* (LAMDA); *Volpone* and *Dr Faustus* (Tangle Theatre).

Omar Austin

Omar trained at Royal Welsh College of Music and Drama.

On graduating, he filmed the second series of Jez Butterworth's *Britannia* for Sky/Amazon, and made his professional stage debut in the world premiere of the new play *God of Chaos* at Theatre Royal, Plymouth.

Other credits include: Pugh in *So Here We Are* (Queen's Theatre, Hornchurch) and Aaron in *The Book of Actions* (Nouveau Riche).

Catriona Faint

Catriona trained at Mountview, graduating in 2020.

Theatre credits include: *The Tempest* (Tron Theatre); *'Tis Pity She's a Whore* (Sam Wanamaker Festival, Shakespeare's Globe); *A Clockwork Orange*, *Emilia*, *Juno and the Paycock* and *Gloria* (Mountview).

Rachael-Rose McLaren

Rachael-Rose trained at RADA, graduating in 2021.

Theatre credits include: *Pomona*, *Consent*, *Spring Awakening*, *King Lear*, *The Bassett Table*, *Ion*, *Twelfth Night* (RADA).

TV and film credits include: *Venus Flytrap* (short film – RADA).

Matthew Pidgeon

National Theatre of Scotland credits include: *The James Plays* (UK and world tour), *The Wonderful World of Dissocia, Realism, Caledonia*.

Other theatre credits include: *The White Card* (Northern Stage/ tour/Soho Theatre); *The Mirror and the Light* (RSC/Gielgud Theatre); *Bitter Wheat* (Garrick Theatre, West End); *Local Hero* (Lyceum Theatre, Edinburgh); *This House* (Chichester/The Garrick/National Theatre/UK tour); *Salome* (RSC); *Wolf Hall* and *Bring Up the Bodies*

(RSC/Aldwych Theatre/Broadway); *Edward II* (National Theatre); *Midsummer* (Traverse Theatre/world tour); *Much Ado About Nothing, The Mysteries* (Shakespeare's Globe); *Kyoto* (Traverse Theatre); *The Lying Kind* (The Royal Court); *The Cherry Orchard, The Wizard of Oz, Vanity Fair, Pinocchio, The Glass Menagerie* (Lyceum Theatre, Edinburgh).

Television credits include: *Life After Life, Crime, Taggart, Casualty, Holby City.*

Film credits include: *Mary Queen of Scots, Daphne, The Winslow Boy, State and Main, A Shot at Glory.*

Radio credits include: *'Tis Pity She's a Whore, Midsummer, Devastated Areas, Kaffir Lillies, The Black Sheep, Mary Stuart, The Cloths of Heaven, Kyoto.*

NATIONAL THEATRE OF SCOTLAND

National Theatre of Scotland is a Theatre Without Walls. We don't have our own building. Instead, we bring theatre to you. From the biggest stages to the smallest community halls, we showcase Scottish culture at home and around the world. We have performed in airports and tower blocks, submarines and swimming pools, telling stories in ways you have never seen before. We want to bring the joy of theatre to everyone. Since we were founded in 2006, we have produced hundreds of shows and toured all over the world. We strive to amplify the voices that need to be heard, tell the stories that need to be told and take work to wherever audiences are to be found.

Artistic Director & Chief Executive: Jackie Wylie

Executive Director: Brenna Hobson

Chair: Jane Spiers

For the latest information on all our activities, visit us online at www. nationaltheatrescotland.com or follow us on:

Twitter @NTSOnline

Facebook @NationalTheatreScotland

YouTube: @ntsonline

Instagram: @ntsonline

SUPPORT NATIONAL THEATRE OF SCOTLAND

Our wonderful donors and supporters help us to:

- Make amazing big shows and wee shows to take all over Scotland, from the grandest theatre stages to the tiniest village halls

- Share stories which reflect the diversity of Scotland – its people, places and history

- Nurture and support Scottish theatre artists

- Reach audiences near and far: on tour, on cinema screens, and across digital platforms

- Create world-class drama and education resources for every school in the country

- Represent Scotland on the international stage

How to support:

- Become a regular Individual Donor

- Corporate Sponsorship

- Introduce us to a Charitable Trust or Foundation

- Remember us in your will

- Attend one of our special fundraising events

Find out more:

Visit www.nationaltheatrescotland.com/support

Contact development@nationaltheatrescotland.com

PITLOCHRY FESTIVAL THEATRE

Since 1951, Pitlochry Festival Theatre has been the artistic heart and soul of Highland Perthshire. Attracting over 100,000 visitors every year, we're more than simply a place to come and see a show – we're Scotland's leading producer of musical theatre, a champion of ensemble practice and the country's only rurally-located, major arts organisation. Our vision is to improve lives by sharing Pitlochry with the world and the world with Pitlochry, and our aim is to create life-enhancing experiences in our theatre and environment – a glorious eleven-acre campus that encompasses the magical Explorers Garden. In everything we do, we are committed to nurturing an exciting creative and cultural future for Scotland.

If there is a definition of a clever man, let it be, he who surrounds himself with the very cleverest women. This play would not be what it is, where it not for the following friends, allies and colleagues:

Caroline Newall
Jackie Wylie
Elizabeth Newman
Rosie Kellagher
Helen Mackay
Charlene Boyd
Garen Unokan
Orla O'Loughlin

I'm forever in your debt. Thank you.

Enough of Him

Characters (4)

Joseph Knight, *late teens*
Ann 'Annie' Thompson, *late teens*
Sir John Wedderburn, *mid forties*
Margaret Wedderburn, *mid twenties*

One

Darkness.

The sound of leather whips being administered savagely against human skin, and a woman cries out for help and in anguish upon every vicious strike.

The lashes and the cries should go on longer than we are comfortable listening to. The whips keep lashing, long after the woman being lashed has stopped crying out in pain.

Two

Early 1770s.

Wedderburn *is ringing an ornate bell. Enter* **Knight** *with a book in his hand.*

Knight *waits for* **Wedderburn** *to turn to him. When* **Wedderburn** *doesn't move:*

Knight   You rang the bell, Sir John?

Wedderburn *opens his eyes and turns to* **Knight**, *noticing the book in his hand.*

Wedderburn   Burning the midnight oil again?

Knight   Guilty.

Wedderburn   May I?

Knight *gives* **Wedderburn** *the book, who skims it.*

Wedderburn   Ah, Plato! So you have finally turned your attention to the Greek philosophers?

Knight   His ideas on the father-son relationship are fascinating to me.

Wedderburn   I was separated from my father young too.

Knight *stares at* **Wedderburn**.

Wedderburn   What?

Knight   It's nothing.

Wedderburn *paces.*

Wedderburn   Now let me see if I remember . . .

'We can easily forgive a child who is afraid of the dark, the real tragedy of life is when men are afraid of the light.'

What do you say to that?

Knight   I haven't got to that part yet.

Beat.

Wedderburn   Is something troubling you?

Knight   I'm just tired.

Wedderburn   You've not been sleeping well?

Knight   I've been sleeping fine.

Wedderburn *offers the book back to* **Knight***, who takes it.*

Wedderburn   Tomorrow is a special day, you know.

Knight   Special how?

Wedderburn   It is the anniversary of the day you came into my service.

Knight   Right.

Wedderburn   You've been part of my household now for . . .

Knight   It's been ten years.

Wedderburn   Look at everything I have achieved in that time. This great house restored, my family status restored.

Knight   You should be very proud.

Wedderburn   I am proud. Of many things. None more so than that I had the good sense about me to ignore all the many offerings Captain John Knight brought to port that day from the Phoenix and insisted on purchasing the quiet boy with the big brown eyes in the corner.

Wedderburn *slaps* **Knight**'s *shoulders and laughs.*

Wedderburn *looks over his shoulder at the door and then turning back to* **Knight** . . .

Wedderburn   Did I not see past the tits and arses and muscles and find a diamond?

Wedderburn *laughs at his joke.*

Knight *laughs too, with much less enthusiasm.*

They settle, and **Wedderburn** *sits.* **Knight** *stays standing.*

Pause.

Wedderburn   You may sit.

Knight   Early day tomorrow, my Lord.

Wedderburn   Right. Of course.

Pause.

Time to retire to bed.

Knight   I think so.

Wedderburn *doesn't move.*

Knight   I expect her Ladyship will be waiting for you.

Wedderburn   Right.

Wedderburn *stands.*

Wedderburn   Good night then, Joseph.

Knight   Goodnight, Sir John.

Three

The dining room. A table.

Enter **Margaret** *and* **Wedderburn**, *behind them* **Knight** *and* **Annie** *stand out of the way.*

Margaret　Good morning.

Wedderburn　Good morning, Margaret. I trust you slept well?

Margaret　I did. Thank you.

Pause.

Margaret　About last night.

Wedderburn　Yes. I –

Margaret　I was expecting you.

Wedderburn　I was talking with Joseph. We got carried away . . . the time, it was very late.

Margaret　You should have woken me.

Wedderburn　I didn't want to disturb you.

Margaret　Yes. I see. I wish you had woken me –

Wedderburn　Shall we?

Wedderburn *leads* **Margaret** *to the table before she can respond, and they both sit.* **Annie** *takes a jug of water and approaches* **Margaret***'s side.*

Margaret　We've received a dinner invitation from the Ogilvy's.

Annie　Water, my Lady?

Margaret *gestures for* **Annie** *to pour.* **Annie** *does so and then approaches* **Wedderburn**.

Wedderburn　Your uncle?

Margaret　Yes.

Annie　Water, my Lord?

Wedderburn *does not respond. He turns to* **Knight**.

Wedderburn　Sit down, Joseph.

Knight   Sorry?

Wedderburn   I said sit down. Join us for breakfast.

Knight *looks between* **Margaret** *and* **Annie**. *Pause.*

Knight   Sir John . . .

Wedderburn *turns to* **Annie**.

Wedderburn   Make way so Joseph can sit down.

Annie *stands back as* **Knight** *sits.* **Wedderburn** *looks at* **Annie**.

Wedderburn   Come along. Pour Joseph some water.

Annie   Apologies.

Annie *pours* **Knight** *some water.*

Annie *stands back. After a beat,* **Knight** *turns back to* **Annie**.

Knight   Thank you.

Annie   You're welcome.

Wedderburn   You must be hungry, Joseph.

Knight   Not really.

Margaret   John?

Wedderburn   I'm starving. What do you want for breakfast?

Knight   I'll have whatever you think is appropriate.

Wedderburn   You will have what we are having then.

Knight *nods.*

Wedderburn *looks to* **Annie** *but before he can speak:*

Margaret   John?

Wedderburn   Yes, Margaret?

Margaret   Don't you think it would be less distracting if Joseph was to eat his breakfast with the servants?

Wedderburn   I have asked my boy to dine with us this morning.

Pause.

Margaret   Yes John, I can see that, but perhaps it would be less confusing for him. And for the other servants.

Wedderburn *turns to* **Annie** *and considers her for a beat. Pause.*

Wedderburn   Stop gawking girl and bring some eggs for Joseph.

Annie   My Lord.

Exit **Annie**.

Knight, **Wedderburn** *and* **Margaret** *linger on for a beat in awkward silence.*

Four

Annie *is washing clothes in a hand basin.*

Enter **Knight**, *who searches through several bags.* **Annie** *watches him.*

Annie   Can I help you, my Lord?

Knight   I'm not a lord.

Annie   You're a servant? Just like me are you? That's funny. I guess it will be my turn to sit down and eat breakfast with his Lord and Ladyship tomorrow then?

Knight *keeps searching.*

Annie   Are you looking for these fancy stockings, Joseph Knight?

Annie *lifts a pair of stockings out of the washing basin.* **Knight** *extends his hand.*

Knight   Give them to me.

Annie I think you'll ask nicely actually. Joseph Knight.

Pause.

Knight Please.

Annie There that wasn't so hard, was it?

Annie *continues washing them.*

Knight I don't have time for this.

Annie Hold your horses. I'm nearly finished.

Knight *waits.*

Eventually **Annie** *wrings them dry, looking them over.*

Annie Maybe you are just like me.

Knight What is that supposed to mean?

Annie Stockings made from silk they may be, but when you look at them really closely, they have holes in them, just like mine.

Annie *laughs, but* **Knight** *remains stony faced.*

Annie You don't like being teased do you, Joseph Knight?

Knight Give me my stockings.

Annie Too big and important to be teased by a lowly maid like me, is that it?

Knight You don't know anything about me.

Annie I know your name. Joseph Knight. Do you know mine?

Knight Thompson. Your name is Thompson.

Annie I have a first name too.

Knight Ann Thompson.

Annie I prefer Annie.

Knight Fine. Annie it is. When we're downstairs.

Annie *laughs to herself.*

Annie   'Only when we're downstairs!'

Annie *throws* **Knight**'s *stockings at him and* **Knight** *catches them / picks them up.* **Annie** *curtseys.*

Annie   It was nice talking to you. My Lord.

Knight *makes to leave, but turns back after a few steps.*

Annie   Yes?

Knight *stares at* **Annie**.

Annie   What's the matter? Cat got your tongue?

Knight *is still staring at* **Annie**. *Off stage a bell rings.*

Annie   Your master's calling.

The bell rings again.

Annie *resumes her washing, singing to herself as she does so.*

Knight *listens to her.*

Annie *looks back up at* **Knight**. *They hold each other's gaze as she sings.*

Knight   That was beautiful.

Pause.

Annie   Do you like to dance Joseph? I like to dance.

Annie *dances, a few simple steps at first. She also sings.*

Enter **Margaret**. *She observes* **Annie** *and* **Knight** *for a beat.* **Knight** *is unable to reciprocate, and stares at the floor.*

Annie *stops – it's awkward.*

Pause.

Margaret   What is the meaning of this?

Knight *and* **Annie** *look to the floor.*

Margaret   This house is not a village hall, is that understood?

Annie   Yes, my Lady.

Margaret *turns her focus to* **Knight**.

Margaret   Is that understood?

Knight *looks at* **Margaret**.

Pause.

Knight   No . . . It is not a village hall.

Pause.

Five

Margaret, **Wedderburn** *and* **Knight** *are sitting at the table eating in silence, with* **Knight** *sitting between* **Wedderburn** *and* **Margaret**.

Margaret *and* **Knight** *look at one another. After a long beat:*

Knight   My Lord –

Wedderburn   Yes, Joseph?

Knight   May I have your permission to travel to Dundee?

Wedderburn   I don't see why not. At the end of the week.

Knight   I would like to go tomorrow.

Margaret   The maids have leave to go to Dundee tomorrow.

Knight   I know, my Lady. If it pleases his Lordship, I would like to travel with them.

Wedderburn   What will you be doing in Dundee?

Pause.

You will tell me the nature of this pressing business if you wish to go.

Wedderburn *looks up from his plate and stares at* **Knight**.

Wedderburn   Well?

Knight   New stockings. I would like to buy new stockings for myself, my Lord.

Margaret   Do the silk stockings he has already chafe too much?

Knight   They do not.

Pause.

Forgive me, Lady Margaret. They do not. But they do have holes in them. The servants do not respect me.

Margaret   I think he should be grateful for his special silk uniform. And be silent.

Throughout this exchange, **Wedderburn** *continues to appraise* **Knight**. *Eventually:*

Wedderburn   You may go to Dundee tomorrow.

Knight   Thank you.

Wedderburn *and* **Knight** *resume eating, while* **Margaret** *stews.*

Margaret   I had to punish one of the maids today.

Wedderburn   Did you?

Margaret   She was absconding from her duties.

Wedderburn   That won't do.

Margaret   Dancing, and singing, as matter of fact. In the washing parlour.

Knight *stops eating.*

Knight   I could think of worse crimes.

Margaret   She should have been doing her duties.

Wedderburn   Quite right.

Margaret   So, you think I was right then. To punish the maid?

Wedderburn   The maid should have been doing her duties. A punishment seems only appropriate. This is a house of rules after all.

Margaret   A house of rules. Yes.

Beat.

I told the girl that for no less than two weeks, she should eat on her own in the library. Without the company of the other maids. And there will be no privileges, like going to Dundee. So that she might reflect on the importance of fulfilling her duties the way this house requires.

Knight   Two weeks?

Margaret *smiles at* **Knight**.

Wedderburn   Perhaps a week would have been enough for a first transgression.

Margaret   Was I too severe?

Wedderburn   No, two weeks is fine.

They all carrying on eating, **Margaret** *and* **Knight** *still eyeing each other.*

Margaret   The man she was dancing with. He should receive two weeks isolation also.

Wedderburn   That seems like fairness. The same punishment for all. Jamaican justice. Right, Joseph?

Margaret   She was dancing with Joseph.

Pause.

What will Joseph's punishment be? He will be punished, won't he?

Pause.

Wedderburn   Leave us now, Joseph.

Knight *doesn't move.*

Wedderburn   Must I always repeat myself?

Knight *exits.*

Margaret   Finally. Just the two of us –

Wedderburn   Do not presume to make a fool of me, woman. Do not presume.

Six

Margaret *is resting on a bedside chair.*

Enter **Annie** *with a foot bath, which she places by the side of the chair and waits.*

Annie   Lady Margaret.

Margaret *does not move.*

Annie   Your bath is ready, Lady Margaret.

Again, **Margaret** *does not move. After a beat,* **Annie** *touches* **Margaret** *on the shoulder.*

Annie   Lady Margaret?

Margaret *removes* **Annie**'s *hand from her shoulder.* **Annie** *steps back and waits.*

After a beat **Margaret** *sits up.*

Margaret   Is it warm?

Annie   I heated the water myself.

Margaret   Go on.

Annie *kneels and takes* **Margaret**'s *foot in her hand.* **Margaret** *kicks out.*

Margaret   What good is warm water if your hands are freezing cold?

Annie *cowers. After a beat:*

Margaret   Give me your hands.

Annie *offers out her hands.* **Margaret** *inspects them.*

Margaret   God have mercy! These hands are filthier than a soldier's feet.

Annie   No there naw.

Margaret   Excuse me?

Annie   Nothing.

Margaret   Never contradict your Lady . . . and never keep her waiting.

Margaret *takes* **Annie**'s *hands in her own hands and rubs them until they are warm.* **Margaret** *releases* **Annie**'s *hands.*

Margaret   There, that's better isn't it? See for yourself.

Margaret *watches* **Annie** *put her hand on her own cheek to check.*

Annie   Thank you.

Margaret *gestures to the foot bath.*

Margaret   Go on.

Annie *bathes* **Margaret**.

Seven

Margaret *is in bed.* **Wedderburn** *is standing, staring at her.*
Silence.

Margaret   The way you are looking at me.

Wedderburn   What of it?

Margaret   There is something about it. Something in your eyes. I find it unsettling.

Pause.

I'd like to know what you are thinking of?

Wedderburn   I'm not thinking of anything.

Margaret   You must be thinking of something.

Wedderburn   I'd like to talk about something else now.

Margaret   So talk. What do you want to talk about?

Pause.

Margaret   I feel like you are punishing me.

Wedderburn   I'm not punishing you.

Margaret   I feel like that is why you keep on inviting your slave to eat with us.

Wedderburn   I have no reason to punish you. Do I?

Margaret   No.

Wedderburn   Then it must be that I am not punishing you.

Pause.

Margaret   John –

Wedderburn   Turn your mind to something else.

Pause.

Margaret   What could make you look at me with such disgust?

Wedderburn   It was not disgust.

Margaret   Shame then?

Wedderburn   That's what you think? That I am ashamed?

Margaret   Yes, that is what that looked like to me.

Pause.

Wedderburn   You are wrong. You could not be more wrong.

Wedderburn *makes to exit but before he can leave:*

Margaret   It is the correct time of the month.

Wedderburn *turns back.*

Wedderburn   I know.

Margaret *gestures to sit.*

Margaret   Come and lie down. Let us try again.

Wedderburn *sits.* **Margaret** *tries to seduce* **Wedderburn**.
Wedderburn *allows her caresses for a beat but then his hands ball
up into fists. He stands.*

Pause.

Margaret   What more can I do? Tell me what I can do.

Wedderburn   Talk less. Try talking less, woman . . . You just
keep talking and talking.

Exit **Margaret**. **Wedderburn** *sits, deep in thought. The light
changes, taking us back to . . .*

Eight

A memory of 1760s Jamaica.

*Bright yellow tropical sunshine, almost too bright and yellow and hot
to be real. The distant sound of tropical birds.*

Knight *is reading. His clothes are very simple.* **Wedderburn**
contemplates him.

Wedderburn   I want you take the rest of the morning off.

Wedderburn *takes the book off* **Knight**.

Wedderburn   You have plenty of time to read in the
evening. That is an order.

Knight *doesn't move.*

Wedderburn   Joseph. What do you do to enjoy yourself?

Knight   I read.

Wedderburn *laughs.*

Wedderburn   One day Joseph, when I am old, and you are wise from reading every book that man has written, I'm going to free you. Then what will you do?

Knight   You would free me?

Wedderburn   Can you imagine it? What a sorry sight you would be. I would wager, the most miserable free man in the whole of Christendom. All that freedom and nothing left for you to read.

Wedderburn *laughs to himself, but* **Knight** *does not.*

Knight   How would I earn that freedom?

Wedderburn   Go for a walk.

Knight   How many years would it take?

Wedderburn   Walk the grounds.

Knight   Three years?

Wedderburn   Allow your mind to wonder.

Knight   Five years?

Wedderburn   Listen to the birds.

Knight   In five years I will be –

Wedderburn   Listen to the birds –

Knight   I will be –

Wedderburn   I said, go for a walk.

Pause.

Knight   Of course. Apologies.

Exit **Knight**.

Nine

Silence.

Annie *is sat by a table eating.*

Enter **Knight**, *who watches* **Annie** *for a beat.* **Annie** *notices* **Knight** *and stands.*

Pause.

Annie   I can leave if you want–

Knight   It's fine.

Annie   I don't want to be in your way.

Knight   You're not . . . I left my book in here.

Knight *points to a book on the table.*

Annie *picks it up and traces her fingers across the book's cover.*

Annie   Sir . . . Will . . . iam . . . B . . . lack . . . sto . . . ne

Annie *looks up at* **Knight**.

Annie   Don't look so surprised. I received my church education just as every other girl did in the parish.

Knight   I meant no offence.

Annie *and* **Knight** *hold each other's gaze.*

Annie   No offence taken.

Knight   Good.

Annie *offers the book to* **Knight**.

Annie   Here you go.

Knight *doesn't take the book, still looking at* **Annie**.

After a beat, **Annie** *puts the book down and collects her things to leave. As she does this:*

Annie   Well, I better be going then. I wouldn't want to delay you from your dinner with the Wedderburn's tonight.

Knight   Do you want to know what it says?

Annie *stops.*

Knight *approaches* **Annie** *and takes the book to find a specific section.* **Knight** *gives it to* **Annie** *and points to the page.*

As **Knight** *recites it word for word,* **Annie** *looks up at him.*

Knight   'There is nothing which so generally strikes the imagination, and engages the affections of mankind, as the right of property; or that sole and despotic dominion which one man claims and exercises over the external things of the world, in total exclusion of the right of any other individual in the universe.'

Pause.

Annie   What other tricks can you do?

Knight   I don't do tricks.

Annie   If I could do tricks like that –

Knight   I don't do tricks.

Pause.

Annie   I wouldn't waste my remembering on boring things. Do you want to know what I'd remember? Things that make you feel in your heart. Not the things that hurt your head, thinking about. I don't suppose you know any things like that, you being Mr. Serious all the time?

Pause.

Knight *is silent for a long beat.* **Annie** *really watches him.*

Knight   I am a child, maybe four, five. The naked soles of my feet are pressed snugly into the white hot sand. My eyes are wide open, looking at the line, the line where heaven touches the earth. Everything is so clear, and the colours of the world feel more real somehow. The yellow ball of fire changes to hues of orange, and then something lighter than an orange, until it merges with the sky, like whiskey dissolving in a glass of water. I see the silhouettes of birds flying home across a sky that is now the colour of red wine; and the sun is half into the water, but its reflection in the lake makes it look complete. Hours pass, but it feels like just a moment until that big ball of yellow has set, giving way to a thousand other smaller dots in the sea of night. In Jamaica. For a slave. Like me. Dancing and singing, laughter even . . . all was forbidden.

Annie   I thought it was because you didn't like me. I thought you might have felt like dancing with someone like me, was beneath you.

Knight *looks back at the door.*

Knight   To be caught doing those things was dangerous. What we could not do with our bodies, we instead learned to do with our minds. And when the sun went down and the masters slept. We told stories . . . stories 'that made your hearts feel', the same way dancing and singing might.

Pause.

Annie *offers out her hand.*

Annie   I can show you. If you like?

Knight *considers* **Annie**, *then takes her hand.*

Annie *slowly repeats the steps she showed* **Knight** *in the washing parlour, this time guiding him.* **Knight** *watches her, entranced.*

Annie *starts to sing as she dances.*

Knight *soon mirrors her movements –* **Annie** *leading as* **Knight** *follows. When they finish,* **Annie** *and* **Knight** *bow/courtesy.*

They hold each other's gaze, before **Annie** *exits.*

Knight *sits, mind full of the past. The light changes like his thoughts and we are in . . .*

Ten

A memory of Jamaica 1760s.

Bright yellow tropical sunshine, almost too bright and yellow and hot to be real. The distant sound of tropical birds.

Enter **Wedderburn** *in simple clothing. He picks the book up off the table.*

Wedderburn   The privation of good.

Pause.

Wedderburn *looks at* **Knight**.

Wedderburn   The privation of good.

Knight   'The privation of good', is a theological doctrine often attributed to St. Augustine of Hippo.

The doctrine states that evil . . .

Pause.

Wedderburn   Continue.

Knight   The doctrine states that evil, unlike good, is insubstantial, so that thinking of it as an entity is misleading. Instead, evil is rather the absence or 'privation' of good. In the way that dark is the absence of light.

Wedderburn   So what does all that mean?

Pause.

Repeating words from a book back to me like a parrot is not the same as learning . . . One is a trick, the other knowledge.

Knight   I know that –

Wedderburn   It means, Joseph, that all perceptions are based on contrast, so that light and dark, good and evil, are imperceptible without each other. Darkness appears only when sources of light are extinguished . . . and the relationship between light and darkness can also be used to frame an understanding of good and evil.

Pause.

Knight   Good and evil are the same as light and darkness?

Wedderburn   Yes.

Knight   Darkness is evil?

Wedderburn   And lightness is good.

Knight   How very convenient.

Wedderburn *laughs, as* **Knight** *looks at his Black skin.*

Knight   So he was saying darkness cannot prevent light?

Wedderburn   Just as evil can offer no resistance to any source of good.

Knight   But –

Wedderburn   St. Augustine of Hippo believed that goodness cannot be actively opposed.

Knight   Yes. But by that logic . . . by that logic evil is normal, evil is always.

Wedderburn *thinks this through for a beat.*

Wedderburn   Good, Joseph. Very good.

Knight   Good is an exception? An effort?

Wedderburn   Yes –

Knight   And without that effort, does that mean that evil will be created out of nothing?

Wedderburn   It is a very bleak view, I agree.

Knight   You cannot truly believe that . . . anymore than you can believe that a man who is dark may fall to sleep one night and, by sheer force of effort, wake up one morning and be white.

Wedderburn *silences* **Knight** *by raising his hand.* **Knight** *obeys.*

Wedderburn   It is just as important in life to know what you disagree with as to know what you agree with. Remember that.

Eleven

Two dressing rooms, either side of the stage. **Margaret** *is being dressed by* **Annie**. **Wedderburn** *is being dressed by* **Knight**.

They continue in silence until both are fully dressed.

Wedderburn *stands in the mirror admiring himself.*

Annie *stops and looks up –* **Margaret** *is staring at her.*

Pause.

Margaret   I'm going to ask you a question, Annie . . . I want you to answer honestly.

Annie   Yes, my Lady.

Margaret   Have you ever known a man?

Annie   I'm not married.

Pause.

Once. When I was younger.

Margaret   Tell me about that.

Annie   There isn't much to tell.

Margaret   Please . . . Please.

Pause.

Annie   What do you want to know?

Margaret   What was it like?

Annie   I was very young. He was old. It wasn't love.

Margaret   Did he enjoy it?

Annie   I think so.

Margaret   You're sure?

Annie *nods.*

Margaret   How are you so sure? He told you perhaps?

Annie *shakes her head.*

Margaret   He never had to?

Annie   No, my lady.

Pause.

Margaret   Did you enjoy it?

Margaret *looks at* **Annie**. *Sees something in her eyes – hesitates.*

Margaret   You didn't enjoy it?

Annie *shakes her head. Almost in tears.*

Pause.

Margaret   Did you have questions? Afterwards? After he had finished with you?

Annie *stares at* **Margaret**. *After a beat.*

Annie   No, my Lady. I did not have any questions.

Pause.

Wedderburn *and* **Margaret** *step forward and we are in –*

Twelve

Wedderburn *and* **Margaret** *stare at each other – either side of a hallway. Behind* **Wedderburn** *is* **Knight**. *Behind* **Margaret** *is* **Annie**.

Margaret *moves to leave.*

Wedderburn   Will you not be joining us for supper?

Margaret *stops.*

Margaret   I shall not.

Pause.

Well, good evening then.

Wedderburn   Good evening.

Exit **Margaret.**

Annie   My Lord.

Annie *exits after* **Margaret.**

Thirteen

Knight *is sat by a table reading.*

Enter **Wedderburn** *with two goblets. He places one by the table near* **Knight.**

Wedderburn *stays standing, staring off.*

Wedderburn   Do you ever think about the past? About Jamaica, Joseph?

Knight   Sometimes.

Wedderburn   I wonder. Do you think a person can forget?

Knight   The past?

Wedderburn   Jamaica.

Knight   I don't know.

Pause.

Wedderburn   I've been dreaming of it of late. Of the markets. It feels vivid, real. Like I was there again for the first time. All that energy, excitement. The smell of it even . . . Sometimes I see the faces of those poor bastards out

there on my brother's plantation. Bodies stripped bare.
Mutilated and left to rot in the sun.

Knight *stops reading, his gaze on* **Wedderburn**.

Wedderburn   Do you ever have problems trying to do your
duty?

Knight   I do what I have to.

Wedderburn   Happy, eh? To be a slave. To have no will. To
make no decisions. Driftwood. How very restful it must be.

Pause.

Wedderburn *looks again into empty space.*

Wedderburn   What now? What now?

Exit **Wedderburn**.

Knight *tears a page out of his book.*

Fourteen

A table.

Knight *is putting the final additions to a toy raft woven together
from tree branches. Enter* **Annie**. *She watches* **Knight** *for a beat as
he takes the page from his book and turns it into a tiny sail.*

Annie   It looks like the beginnings of a boat.

Knight   A raft, you mean.

As he carries on working:

It's something I used to do as a child. I'd build these
out of –

Annie   Sugar cane?

Knight   Do I look like I had a death wish?

Annie *smiles.*

Annie *and* **Knight** *look down at the 'raft'.*

Knight   So where are we sailing to?

Annie   I don't know, Joseph.

Knight   The game can't start until you decide where we are sailing.

Annie   You decide. You can tell me all about it.

Knight   I want you to decide.

Knight *waits for her to think of an answer.*

You decided, yet?

Pause.

Annie   How about . . . everywhere?

Knight   Everywhere isn't a place. You have to be more specific. Try again.

Pause.

Annie *makes to exit, but before she can* **Knight** *calls after her:*

Knight   Do you not want to play anymore?

Annie   Is that what you're doing? Playing? Is making me feel stupid a game to you?

Knight   Making you feel stupid? How?

Annie   I can't imagine like you, Joseph.

Knight   Of course you can.

Annie   I've never been outside Perthshire.

Knight   You can read. Anybody that can read can imagine.

Annie   I can read, yes. But that doesn't mean I've got big worlds inside my head like you.

Knight *holds out his hand, and after a long moment,* **Annie** *takes it.* **Knight** *leads* **Annie** *over to the table. She sits. he places the raft in her hands.*

Knight   Close your eyes, Annie.

Annie *does so.* **Knight** *is silent for a while.*

Knight   Have you ever seen the sea before?

Annie   I've seen the River Tay, by Port Dundee.

Knight   Try and remember the sound of it. The sound of the water moving, the crashing of the waves. Can you hear it in your head?

We hear the sound of the sea as **Annie** *does – it is magical.*

Annie   I can hear it.

Knight   Good. Hold on to that sound. That is what the ocean sounds like. It's just water, just like the River Tay, but it's bigger, so vast it might be everlasting. And crossing the ocean, can you see a wooden ship so small it seems it is travelling the length of the world? And that's you on that ship, can you see yourself?

Annie   I think so. What can I smell? What am I standing on? What's beneath my feet ? –

Knight   Forget about the darkness below you . . . just look ahead of you. Right at the front of the ship, that's where you are. You can see sunlight glistening on the waves like a promise of hope.

Open water is so beautiful, but you've been out at sea for so long now that you long to be on land again. And there it is, way ahead but drawing closer. A cheer goes up from the sailors behind you as the ship ploughs towards Kingston Harbour. It's all tall masted frigates, and dock workers scurrying around like bees on a honey comb. The harbour has a bewildering beauty.

Annie *opens her eyes, breathless.*

Annie   I wish I had seen half the things that you've seen.

Knight   No, you don't.

Annie   Don't I? When I close my eyes, I don't see oceans and beauty. I see people living their small lives in small cottages, tilling their small patch of land. I see them with their dirty hands and old ragged clothes. I see the same burns, and the same tatty fields, that's all I can see . . .

Knight   It's not all oceans and paradises in my head.

Fifteen

A memory of Jamaica 1760s.

Bright yellow tropical sunshine, almost too bright and yellow and hot to be real. The distant sound of tropical birds.

Wedderburn *is standing in a simple shirt, covered in blood. He tries to wipe at the blood but it won't come out.*

Wedderburn   Joseph.

Wedderburn *calls out again but louder.*

Joseph!

After a long beat, enter **Knight**, *also dressed simply.*

Wedderburn   Joseph . . .

Wedderburn *trails off upon seeing that* **Knight** *is here. They stare at each other.*

Pause.

Knight   Who was it this time?

Wedderburn   The girl. Livia.

Knight *exits, and returns with a bucket filled with water and a cloth, which he uses to clean the blood off* **Wedderburn**.

Knight *takes* **Wedderburn**'s *shirt off then dresses him with fresh clothes.*

Pause.

Knight   Will she live?

Wedderburn *and* **Knight** *stare at each other.*

Sixteen

Wedderburn *and* **Knight** *sit facing one another over a chess board.* **Annie** *stands back, waiting to reset the table.*

Wedderburn *studies the board for a long time.*

Wedderburn *finally touches a pawn, considers moving it, and then withdraws his hand, thinking better of it.*

Knight *sighs.*

Wedderburn   Am I keeping you from some pressing matter, Joseph?

Wedderburn *continues studying the board.*

You have played tonight like a man who fears there will be no tomorrow.

Knight   Yes, and you have played like a man for whom the day is ever endless and the night always at bay.

Wedderburn *seizes a piece with intent and makes his move.*

Wedderburn   You place too much value on the lesser pieces.

Wedderburn *looks up from the board at* **Knight** *and finally notices that he is distracted. He turns to see* **Annie**.

Pause.

Wedderburn   Am I boring you, Joseph?

Knight *turns his attention back to the board.*

Wedderburn   Perhaps you would have Miss Thompson come and take your place at the table instead?

Knight *continues to focus on the table. After a beat he seizes a chess piece and makes his move.*

Wedderburn *assesses the table.*

Knight   You once promised me that I could go free.

Wedderburn   I did?

Knight   You said after so many years.

Wedderburn   I did say something like that.

Knight   I was thinking perhaps we should make a contract. Write it down. You wouldn't object to that, would you?

Wedderburn   Do you not trust me to keep my word?

Knight   Of course I trust you.

Wedderburn   Then why do you need a contract?

Knight   It's the proper thing to do.

Wedderburn   Yes but why now?

Knight   I just want to know where I stand.

Wedderburn *looks up from the board at* **Knight**.

Pause.

Wedderburn   Your timing. It's curious.

Knight   How so?

Wedderburn   I read a story yesterday in the newspaper about a slave called Somerset. Perhaps you have seen it also, Joseph?

Knight   I have seen it, yes.

Wedderburn   Ah.

Knight   What does that mean, 'Ah'?

Pause.

Knight   The Somerset case is not the reason why I ask . . .

Wedderburn   Of course not, Joseph. It's just an unhappy coincidence that your request coincides with this reckless reporting that Mansfield is going to side with the slave.

Knight   It is just that, a coincidence.

Wedderburn *thinks on this for a beat.*

Wedderburn   His master, Charles Stewart won't allow it to stand.

Wedderburn *holds* **Knight**'s *stare for a long beat.*

Pause.

Knight   And if it was you in Stewart's position? And me in Somerset's . . . things would be different. Wouldn't they?

Wedderburn *returns to assessing the table.*

Knight   Wouldn't they?

They carry on in this silence.

After a long beat, **Knight** *stands and exits.* **Wedderburn** *leans back in his chair.*

Pause.

Wedderburn   Thompson?

Annie *comes over to* **Wedderburn***, and waits.*

Annie   My Lord?

Wedderburn *doesn't respond for a long beat.*

Wedderburn   I notice you have been spending time with Joseph Knight.

Annie   Not when I should be working.

Wedderburn   I'm told most nights. Am I under the wrong impression?

Pause.

Wedderburn *sits down.*

Annie   Some nights. After I have finished my duties.

Wedderburn   What do you talk about?

Annie   Books.

Wedderburn *laughs.*

Wedderburn   Such as?

Pause.

Wedderburn *stands and gets in* **Annie**'s *personal space, looking at her for an uncomfortably long time.*

Annie   We once talked about a Blackstone, my Lord.

Wedderburn   William Blackstone?

Annie   Yes, my Lord.

Pause.

Wedderburn   And what else do you talk about with my Joseph?

Pause.

Annie   We sometimes talk about the past. About his past. Never about you. Just about his past.

Pause.

Wedderburn   Ah, you're a clever girl, aren't you? Careful not to say the wrong words.

Annie   I wouldn't know, my Lord. Can I please go back to my duties now?

Wedderburn   You'll resume your duties when I tell you to.

Pause.

Wedderburn *steps back from* **Annie**'s *space.*

Wedderburn   Well? Let us hear it then. What does Joseph say about his past to lowly Annie Thompson?

Pause.

Speak, and you may return to your duties.

Pause.

Annie   Lightning strikes. A storm thrashes. The ocean is all turmoil –

Wedderburn   Damn you, woman! Speak up!

Annie *regains her composure, becoming more fluent and confident as she continues.*

Annie   Lightning strikes. A storm thrashes. The ocean is all turmoil. The ship is tossed hopelessly but you feel safe from the storm, in this room. No one comes and goes, no one but the Captain. The door crashes open. It's HIM. He takes off his coat and sits down on the bed. 'Come here boy,' he says. You walk over to him. He grabs hold of your wrists and pushes you down onto the bed. You start to breathe heavily . . .

Then the ship rocks suddenly, and he flies forward and bangs his head on the wall. He is dazed. You run out of the room, out into the storm – one sailor calls out to you, 'Hold!' just as you disappear beneath the deck. Below the deck now, you do your best to move beyond the naked bodies chained together; they cry and moan, huddled together in the dark.

A naked woman reaches out to you. Something about her reminds you of your mother. A disturbing stillness to her: 'I will die out here,' she says. You reach out to her, to comfort her. The sailor who shouted 'hold' is stood behind you now; he is carrying a whip. 'There you are!' he says and raises his hand. But before he can strike you, the captain comes down and shouts 'Don't!'

He comes to you as the sailor lowers his hand and hugs you to HIM. An act of kindness. It feels like kindness. The look on the woman's face has changed. He takes your hand and leads you back above deck; you go with HIM. On your way up, you see the look on every other slave's face as you leave. It is the same as the woman: shame, pity, disgust. You know then that you're not 'one of them'.

Pause.

Wedderburn   You may go back to your duties.

Annie *stares at* **Wedderburn**.

Wedderburn   Move from my sight.

Exit **Annie**. **Wedderburn** *stares out into space.*

Seventeen

Margaret *is sat on a chair brushing her hair with a beautiful ornate hairbrush. Enter* **Wedderburn**.

After a beat:

Wedderburn   Tell me something, Margaret. Have I just seen Ann Thompson upstairs?

Margaret   She has been assisting me.

Wedderburn   Where is your usual chamber maid?

Margaret   Her child has taken sick. I gave her leave to her parents' cottage in Dundee until the child is recovered.

Wedderburn   You have promoted Ann Thompson then?

Margaret   Are you unhappy with how I run this house?

Wedderburn   Far from it.

Pause.

Margaret   Will you be joining me this evening?

Wedderburn   No, I think not.

Margaret   It's the correct time of the month.

Wedderburn   Well then. I guess that settles it.

Margaret   Please don't sound too excited.

Margaret *stops brushing her hair.*

Pause.

Shall we then?

Wedderburn *and* **Margaret** *start undressing, miserably.*

Margaret   In Jamaica . . . I'm sure your life was very different in Jamaica –

Wedderburn   You have no business asking me about Jamaica.

Pause.

Margaret   So did you have relations then, with your slaves?

Wedderburn   When you became my legal wife you agreed to this understanding, not to discuss Jamaica. You have no business asking me about bedwarmers.

Wedderburn *moves to exit.*

Margaret   Is that what you were thinking about? When the way you looked at me unsettled me so much. Your bed warmers?

Wedderburn *stops.*

Wedderburn   God save me from such stupid questions.

Wedderburn *turns back to* **Margaret**.

Wedderburn   For the last time Margaret, I was not thinking of anything.

Wedderburn *approaches* **Margaret**. *She retreats.*

Wedderburn   Is that understood?

Margaret *stares at* **Wedderburn**.

Margaret   How many?

Tell me how many.

Wedderburn   Several. I had several bedwarmers. Are you happy now?

Margaret   I will be happy when we have done our duty and had our children.

Pause.

Did you ever have these . . . difficulties –

Wedderburn   I'm not having difficulties.

Margaret   – with them? With your . . . bedwarmers . . . in Jamaica . . .?

Wedderburn   I'm not having difficulties.

Margaret *stares at* **Wedderburn.**

Wedderburn   No. No I did not.

Margaret *looks crestfallen.*

Pause.

Wedderburn   Forgive me. You push too hard, Margaret. Why must you always push so hard?

Pause.

Margaret   Do I not appeal to you?

Wedderburn   You do.

Margaret   Tell me. What is it you did with them?

Pause.

Wedderburn   It was different. With different slaves.

Margaret   Yes, I'm sure that's true. No one person can be exactly the same.

Pause.

There was nothing that you particularly liked?

Wedderburn *walks off.*

Pause.

Wedderburn   Well . . .

I liked to watch them crawl upon their hands and knees.

And I liked them to be silent. Deathly silent. I didn't even like to hear them breathing.

Wedderburn *stares at* **Margaret.**

Wedderburn   I liked them to lick my feet.

One time I whipped a . . .

Margaret   Go on.

Wedderburn   The first time I whipped a female slave, I thought I knew how such a thing would make me feel. Sad? Disturbed, perhaps? But no. As the skin peeled off her flesh, I did not feel any of those feelings. I felt alive, I felt full of life and with every crashing whip, I felt aroused

Silence.

Wedderburn *sits down. Exhales.*

Margaret, *stunned, watches him for a long beat. Eventually:*

Margaret   Look at me.

Wedderburn *ignores her.*

Margaret   Please look at me.

Wedderburn *looks at* **Margaret. Margaret** *gets on her knees.*

Margaret   Would it help. If you were cruel to me?

Wedderburn   I can't do that.

Margaret   You mean you won't?

Wedderburn   You do not know what you are asking of me.

Margaret   I am asking you to use me like you would them.

Wedderburn   I will not.

Margaret   Why not? Why not, John?

We have our duty as husband and wife.

Wedderburn   That I would use you as some Black bitch in Jamaica? Because I find the idea repulsive.

And you should find it repulsive too.

Eighteen

Annie's *bedroom*

Enter **Knight** *and* **Annie**.

Annie   Lock the door, Joseph.

Knight *considers this for a beat, then does as he is asked.*

Annie   Keep your back turned.

Knight   What?

Knight *faces the door, waiting.*

Annie *opens a cupboard door, standing behind it so* **Knight** *can't see her. She takes off her cap. And ties a ribbon in her hair.*

Annie   I hope you're not looking.

Knight   I wouldn't dare.

Knight *hears* **Annie** *approach.*

Annie   You can look now.

Knight *turns to face her.*

Annie   Do you like it?

Annie *and* **Knight** *stare at each other for several long moments.*

Annie   There's something I need to tell you Joseph.

Pause.

I'm with child.

Knight *starts laughing, softly at first but then a much more full bodied laughter*

Annie   So you're happy then?

Knight   Happy? Am I happy? One day soon, Annie Thompson, when I am free and we are away from this house, I'm going to marry you.

Annie   So you want to marry me now?

Knight *sticks out his hand.* **Annie** *takes it.*

Annie *and* **Knight** *dance.*

A bell rings somewhere else in the house.

Annie   You better get going.

Knight   I do. I do want to marry you.

The bell rings again.

Annie   Don't keep him waiting, Joseph.

The bell rings again. **Knight** *and* **Annie** *finish,* **Knight** *steps back and takes* **Annie** *in for a long beat until –*

Annie   Joseph. Go.

The bell rings again and again and again. Exit **Knight**.

Nineteen

Wedderburn *is sitting at the chess board, waiting. He has been waiting for some time. Just as* **Wedderburn** *is reaching to ring his bell again, enter* **Knight**. *He does not sit.*

Wedderburn   You're late.

Knight   If it pleases you, we might play another evening?

Wedderburn   It doesn't please me. Sit down, Joseph.

Pause.

I have moved. Rook to King, Bishop three.

Knight *sits, but looks directly at* **Wedderburn**.

Wedderburn   Perhaps you might try looking at the table.

Knight *continues to look at* **Wedderburn**. *Eventually,* **Knight** *moves and captures a piece of* **Wedderburn**'s.

Wedderburn *sighs.*

Wedderburn   You're not improving.

Wedderburn *makes another move quickly.*

I would like to know the reason it took you so long to answer my call just now . . .

Pause.

Did you not hear the bell ringing?

Knight   I heard it.

Wedderburn   I rang several times.

Knight   I lost myself in a book.

Wedderburn   You were reading?

Knight   That's right.

Wedderburn   You were in the library then?

Pause.

Knight   No. I wasn't in the library.

Wedderburn   No, you weren't.

Knight   You sent a servant there to fetch me when I didn't respond.

Wedderburn   Not just to the library, Joseph.

I'll only ask you one more time. The reason it took you so long to come to my call?

Pause.

Knight *stands.*

Wedderburn   Sit down.

Knight   I don't want to play anymore.

Wedderburn   I said sit down.

Knight *sits.*

Wedderburn   It's because of that woman, isn't it?

Knight   I don't know what you are talking about.

Wedderburn   You will answer me. Or I will ask that whore myself.

Knight *sweeps his hand across the table so the pieces scatter everywhere, and the board falls to the floor.*

Pause.

Wedderburn *stands, towering above* **Knight** *who is sat down; he looks every inch the Jamaican master, ready to dominate his slave.*

After a beat **Knight** *stands, looking* **Wedderburn** *in the eyes.*

The two men square up to one another. If we didn't know any better, we would be hard pressed to know which man played the role of the father and master and which man played role of the son and the slave.

Wedderburn   If we were in Jamaica, I would be obliged to punish you for those actions.

Knight   We are not in Jamaica.

Wedderburn   Do you have nothing more to say to me? No words of contrition? Do you not even have it in you to apologise?

Knight   I will not apologise.

Pause.

Wedderburn   Has it always been so unbearable for you to serve me?

Knight   Not always.

Wedderburn   But it is unbearable for you now?

Pause.

Knight   You had me come to you once. Some months ago. To this room. I had just started reading the Greek philosophers. Plato. You remember?

Wedderburn   I do.

Knight   You spoke to me of a common ground between us. That we had both lost our fathers at a young age.

Wedderburn   This? This is why your life with me is so unbearable? Because of my generosity?

Knight   I looked in your face that day. I could see in your eyes as plain as I could read the words on the page, that you genuinely believe my loss and your loss are the same. Because of your generosity. I said nothing. I always say nothing. I'm so tired of saying nothing . . . We are not the same. We are not the same. Your loss of your father in war and my kidnap and enslavement and removal from my father are as different as night and day. To keep that part of me silent. That is what is unbearable. That is why I must be free.

Exit **Knight**.

Twenty

The **Wedderburn** *bedroom.*

Margaret *sits on the edge of the bed. Enter* **Annie**.

Margaret *takes out an ivory hairbrush.*

Margaret   My hair looks a mess.

Annie   That's a fine brush you have there.

Pause.

Margaret *looks long and hard at* **Annie**.

Margaret   It was my mother's.

Margaret *hands over the ivory brush.* **Annie** *inspects it.*

Margaret   You can brush my hair with it if you like?

Annie   Yes, my Lady.

Annie *brushes* **Margaret**'s *hair. After a moment of this:*

Annie   You said your mother left you it?

Margaret   When she died. She left me this brush, and certain responsibilities. Look after my father and his dogs.

Annie   That sounds like a lot.

Margaret   It was. My father was a handful.

Annie   They all are . . . Fathers, I mean.

Margaret   He was a solider. David Ogilvy. In his regiment, they called him 'Le Bel Écossais'.

Annie   That's got a nice ring to it.

Margaret   It means 'the beautiful Scotsman'.

Annie   He must have been a great man. To have such a name.

Annie *and* **Margaret** *laugh together.*

Pause.

Margaret   Do you know what Jamaica is, Annie?

Annie   A place at the other side of the world.

Margaret   Yes.

Annie   A place that's warm.

Margaret   That too.

Pause.

Margaret   I think Jamaica is . . . a perfect Babylon.

Pause.

Margaret   My husband went there at eighteen. Of course Joseph Knight became a man there too.

Annie *deliberately pulls the brush roughly through* **Margaret**'s *hair.*

Margaret   OW!

Annie   I'm terribly sorry, my Lady.

Annie *moves to brush* **Margaret**'s *hair again.*

Margaret   I think that will be enough brushing for one evening.

Pause.

Annie *moves to leave.*

Margaret   How is he with you?

Annie *stops.*

Annie   Who, my Lady?

Margaret *looks at* **Annie**.

Pause.

Annie   I don't know what you mean, my Lady.

Margaret   These walls have ears, Annie. Secrets never keep.

Annie   I don't know what anyone has said, my Lady but –

Margaret   Your child will need providing for. Your child with Joseph.

Pause.

I would see a better outcome for you, Annie. Not this sad, miserable –

Annie   I'm not sad like you.

I'm sorry, my Lady. I know you are sad. And there is not a day that goes by that I do not pity you for it. But I am not.

Pause.

Annie   I know you think you mean well, my Lady, but I would not be so desperately cleaved to some unkind benefactor the way Joseph is to his Lordship.

Margaret   You call me unkind?

Annie   See now how your beady eyes stare at me for saying a simple truth – that what you want is not what I want.

Margaret   I just want you to be happy –

Annie   Big people like you, you only understand the happiness of small people like me if their every breath is one of gratitude to your generosity. I'm touched by your offer, my Lady. But I shall not be parted from Joseph.

Pause.

Margaret   If you are right about him, then I envy you Annie Thompson . . . I envy you so very much.

Annie   I am right.

Margaret *and* **Annie** *stare at each other but* **Annie** *looks away first – a hint of doubt. Enter* **Wedderburn**. **Margaret** *notices him.*

Wedderburn   Leave us.

Annie *faces* **Wedderburn**.

Margaret   We are not finished.

Wedderburn   I will not ask again.

Pause.

Margaret *backs down. She hugs* **Annie**.

Margaret *turns to leave the room.*

Annie   Lady Margaret.

Margaret *stops and* **Annie** *offers* **Margaret** *the brush.*

Margaret   No, you keep it. It's yours now.

Exit **Margaret**.

Pause.

Wedderburn   You may sit.

Annie   I would rather stand.

Twenty-One

A bare table.

Enter **Knight**, *who looks around the room he has spent so much time in, both happy and sad.*

Knight *picks up* **Wedderburn**'s *bell and sits at the head of the table –* **Wedderburn**'s *usual seat.*

Knight *rings the bell and waits. Silence.*

Knight *rings the bell for long this time. No response again.* **Knight** *rings the bell without stopping this time.*

Enter **Margaret**. **Knight** *sees her but keeps ringing.* **Wedderburn** *finally enters.*

Wedderburn   What is the meaning of this?

Knight *is still ringing the bell.* **Wedderburn** *takes it from him.*

Wedderburn   Have you lost your mind, boy?

Pause.

Wedderburn   Have you lost your mind?

Wedderburn *puts the bell down.*

Pause.

Wedderburn   Fine. Fine. Let us all return to bed. We will discuss this in the morning –

Knight   All my life you have seemed so very big to me, do you know that? Today all I see is a small, bitter, ugly, mean person. You dismissed Annie?

Wedderburn   I have made a generous offer. Your bastard . . . your child will be provided for.

Knight   You promised me that I could go free. I ask you now to honour that promise.

Wedderburn   Not today.

Knight   I am to be a father in six months.

Wedderburn   Whose fault is that? Did I tell you to lie with that woman?

Knight   Sir John, you don't mean 'not today'. You mean: 'just not for her'.

Wedderburn   Do you call me a liar now? In my own house, you call me a liar? You ungrateful bastard!

Pause.

Am I missing something here, Joseph? Have I not been a force for good inside your life?

Knight   Listen, John –

Wedderburn   Enough now, Joseph. Go to bed. Go to bed before you say something that can not be taken back.

Knight *does not move.*

Pause.

Wedderburn   I have always tried my best not to ever treat you like a slave. No honest man could accuse me of treating you as low as that. Not since we came back here to Scotland. And no other man has ever treated you as a slave. Because I haven't let them, Joseph. I have protected you. And this, this is my reward? John? Who are you to address me as John?

Knight   I am a man. My name is Joseph. And your name is John.

Wedderburn   You're not a man, Joseph. You're a slave. You're my property. That can not change.

Pause.

Wedderburn *walks off to compose himself. After a beat:*

Margaret   What if he asked for less than freedom?

Wedderburn *and* **Knight** *turn to* **Margaret**.

Margaret   The unused servant's cottages, the ones in disrepair. Annie could stay there permanently. Joseph could continue his service –

Wedderburn   And in this arrangement, my providing a lifelong home for Annie Thompson and her child, on my grounds, this would be what?

Knight   A gift. A generous gift.

Wedderburn   No, Joseph. Not a gift. A price for your loyalty. You would be bought then like a common whore?

Knight   A price worth paying for my child.

Wedderburn   So it is a fee that you are asking for now? You think I should pay for your loyalty? Have I not been generous enough? All these requests, they come from her instruction. Yes, I see your mouth moving, but it is that woman's voice I hear coming out from those Black lips.

You think that I don't know what you feel? Yes, I know. You felt the veins and flesh and warmth between a white woman's thighs and the irony is, she has made a slave out of you where I had made you free.

Margaret   John –

Wedderburn   My answer is no.

Knight   Free or not, I will marry the one I love.

Wedderburn *laughs. He laughs and laughs.*

Margaret   Stop this.

Wedderburn   Don't be so ridiculous, Joseph. People don't marry for love.

Margaret   Stop this.

Wedderburn   They marry for position, they marry for status, they marry for security. Is that what you think, that she loves you?

Wedderburn *laughs again.*

Margaret   STOP THIS MADNESS NOW.

Silence.

Nothing good can come from this.

Wedderburn   I have been a good man to him.

Wedderburn *turns to* **Knight**.

Wedderburn   To you. I have been a good man. Why can you no longer recognise that?

Margaret   He does recognise that. Don't you? Tell him that you recognise that, Joseph . . .

Knight *says nothing.*

Wedderburn   That woman will not be staying in the disused cottages.

Pause.

I mean, how can I accept such a thing. After she has betrayed this house?

Knight   What betrayal do you speak of now?

Wedderburn   Some valuable items of Margaret's have gone missing. An ivory brush.

Wedderburn *looks to* **Margaret**, *as does* **Knight**.

Knight   Annie is no thief.

Wedderburn   Do not badger my wife.

Knight   You owe her more than this.

Pause.

Wedderburn   Well then –

Margaret   Annie Thompson is not a thief.

Wedderburn   Margaret –

Margaret   She is not a thief, John.

Pause.

Wedderburn   This has clearly been a trying episode for you to witness. Perhaps you might retire to your room.

Margaret   I will not. And I will not stand false witness against my maid. She is a good and honest woman. She is not a thief.

Wedderburn   Margaret, you have forgotten yourself.

Margaret   No, I have found myself.

Wedderburn   You are my wife. And you will obey me and be silent.

Margaret   I am your wife. But it is not me but you who has forgotten themselves.

Wedderburn *slams his hand on the table.*

Wedderburn   Go to bed. I command you to go to bed.

Margaret *slams her hand on the table right back at him.*

Margaret   You go to bed.

Wedderburn   This conversation is over. Over! Finished! We are done with this!

Silence.

Knight   Sir John –

Wedderburn *grabs* **Knight** *by the throat.* **Knight** *stands his ground.*

Wedderburn   Do not mistake my kindness for weakness.

Wedderburn *realises himself and releases* **Knight**. *A long pause.*

Wedderburn   Look what you've made me do . . . Look what you've made me do.

Exit **Wedderburn**.

Pause.

Margaret *approaches* **Knight**, *but he raises his hand to stop her.*

Knight   Do not touch me.

Pause.

Margaret   He'll never understand.

Knight *and* **Margaret** *really see each other.*

Margaret   What will you do now?

Knight *straightens his jacket.*

Knight   Run.

Margaret   Good luck, Joseph Knight.

Exit **Margaret**.

Knight *carefully takes off his silk uniform, and changes into very simple, much less ornate clothing and sings.*

As he does so, we hear some clips of the words that will eventually be the famous decision of Sheriff **John Swinton**. *Sounds of a chaotic and busy courtroom.*

Swinton   It is a great question. Does a Black, the moment he sets foot upon British ground, become immediately free?

During this case, I have considered a number of authorities put forward in support of the opinion that slavery was no new thing; that the Romans, those great friends to liberty, understood it well; that even in Scotland in the year 1258 slaves and their children were conveyed from one master to another, in the same manner that sheep and horses are now.

(*Steely-eyed.*) Let me be clear, it is this court's opinion that slavery at this day is authorised by the legislator of Great Britain.

In such Jamaican circumstances, our law is transparent and unequivocal.

To quote authorities from the practice of ancient nations, or even from that of our own country in the more early periods of her history, any advocate could have no difficulty in producing an equal number of authorities in support of every one crime of which human nature is capable.

He raises his voice over the sounds of a chaotic court.

The presumption of law must be in favour of liberty.

Several courts of justice in Europe have rejected the claim of slavery with indignation.

The great Judge Holt had said well 'that English air was too pure for a slave to breathe', and Lord Mansfield has given a liberal decision in the famous case of Somerset.

It is my opinion that the state of slavery is not recognised by the laws of this kingdom, and is inconsistent with the principles thereof. Further, that the regulations in Jamaica concerning slaves do not extend to this kingdom. I find in favour of the Pursuer and overturn the decision of the lower court.

SUDDEN CHANGE LIGHT And we are in . . .

Twenty-Two

Dundee, 1775.

Outside a small cottage.

That beautiful Scottish light that comes just before dawn, perfectly in between the true dark of night and the full light of day.

Knight *stands looking out into the dark.*

Annie (*offstage*)   Joseph. Joseph, where are you? Joseph?

After a beat, enter **Annie**, *trailing off as she sees him.*

Annie   Joseph.

Annie *stands some way behind* **Knight**. *She looks beyond him for a moment, and then turns to leave.*

Knight   Don't go.

Annie *stops.*

Annie   It's too early, Joseph.

Knight   I know. I'm just –

Annie   Being stupid?

Knight   I'm trying to say I'm so –

Annie   You're sorry.

Knight   Maybe if you let me speak.

Pause.

Have you ever noticed how dark it is?

Annie   What?

Knight   Out here in Dundee. It's darker somehow. And Colder. At the Wedderburns' . . . it was never dark, was it? There was always something, some candle or fire in the hearth.

Annie *kneels to pick up some leaves from the ground and smell them. It's nice – she did this as a young girl.*

Annie   God, this place.

Knight   What about it?

Annie   Being back out here. I sometimes forget how every corner of this place reminds me of my father. Him drinking. Agitating for a fight, following me around the place the way he always did. Last time I saw him, just before I left for Ballindean, I told him to go and fuck himself. And he says to me, 'go out into the woods and find a stick. And it better be a big stick. A strong stick'. 'Why?' I asked? 'Why do you want a stick, father?' 'Because I'm going to kill you with it'.

Knight   What did you do?

Annie   I went out into the woods.

Knight   You actually got the stick?

Annie   I gave him the biggest piece of wood I could find and I said to him, 'Go on then'.

Pause.

Knight   I'm sorry I wasn't there with you then.

Annie   Me too.

Pause.

Sir John always reminded me of him, my father. That condescending look in his eye, like I had disappointed him by just daring to breathe the same air.

Knight   Is that why you hated him so much?

Annie   I hated him because of what he did to you, Joseph.

Knight *considers the papers in his hand.*

Knight   He wrote to me. Margaret Wedderburn has passed away.

Pause.

Annie   Did he say how she died?

Knight   There were some complications after the birth of their son.

Annie   Oh.

Did she suffer?

Knight   It doesn't say.

Pause.

I have this picture in my mind of him roaming around those hallways, lost and alone and angry and sad. With no one there to be there for him.

Annie   Are you that broken, that everything has to be about him?

Knight   You know I'm tired –

Annie   Yes, well, I'm tired too –

Knight   I'm tired of you . . . I'm tired of you feeling sorry for me. Like I had it so bad! I didn't have it so bad. Definitely not in Jamaica. Plenty of people had it worse. But in his house, in Ballindean, I had respect, and I never wanted for nice things –

Annie   Nice things? You were his nice thing.

I'm tired of all this standing outside on your own in the dark. Joseph, we have lost too.

Knight *looks at* **Annie**.

Knight   I wanted you to have that baby so much.

Anne   I know.

Knight   I wanted to be a father as much as you wanted to be a mother.

I wanted it so much. I wanted it so so much.

Annie   I know Joseph. I know.

Pause.

I don't know how to make you happy anymore, Joseph.

Knight   It's not your fault.

Annie   Some days I wake up in a cold sweat, and I roll over, and you're not there next to me. And I ask myself is this the day that he just walks away. I mean, I've got nothing to offer you.

Knight   You've got plenty to offer me.

Annie   Then why are you so restless?

Knight   Maybe I am broken. Maybe that's why I stand out here in the dark. After everything we've been through, after all these years, I'm stood out here and all I can think of is some stupid thing he said to me once when he was in Jamaica about listening to the birds. It's like however far or fast I run, this chain will run with me. Even if the courts of law have said I am free, free to go how I please, free to be with who I love, I'm not free inside here. I look around myself and I want to scream because it feels like nothing has changed.

Pause.

I don't want to feel like I wish I never met you. I want to look upon your face and just feel good, you know? But I've been robbed of that. That simple pleasure.

Knight *stands there, helpless.*

Annie *tries to go to him, but he puts his hand out to tell her to stop – as he tries desperately to hold it together.*

Annie *talks as she edges closer to* **Knight**.

Annie   For so many years I felt like I'd been waiting, waiting for some crystal clear moment, when all the grey clouds overhead would disappear. The day I moved out of this cottage, I still felt it inside. That pain. And then I got the job in Ballindean. Still nothing. And then my father died, and I was sure that, that would be the day that I would feel better. Still nothing. And then I met you.

Knight   Why can't I be free? Why can't I just be free?

Annie *holds him close.*

Knight *holds her right back.*

As they stand there together and the sun starts to rise, we hear it nearby – the sound of Scottish birdsong. The notes are simple yet somehow hold so much.

9 781350 377752